The Language of Daisies

M.B.Victoria

ISBN-13: 978-1-098-78441-6

M.B.P., I thank you and I miss you.

Mom and Pop, always.

Content

Madness... *3*

Journey... *47*

Passion... *95*

Home... *139*

Listen carefully
to the language of daisies.
They know to move
with the breeze and not against it.

The daisies know that darkness will pass
because the sun always rises,
and they know to face the sun when it comes,
so as not to drown out in the shadows.

They know that
there is no point in crying when the sky cries
because growth comes with the rain
and growth simply isn't possible without it.

The daisies know that
the only way to survive a storm
is to trust in the knowledge that
their roots run deep.

They know that there must be a balance
between standing firm and moving at the will of the wind,
so listen carefully as the daisies might just be able to
share with you the language they so lovingly speak.

Madness

How difficult it is
to be the victim
of your own madness.

Find the Worth

I don't like speaking
about what has hurt,
but oh I must,
I must, and I must
because my pain carries with it
lessons learned.

If I can share my story
and reach someone
along the way,
then at least I can say
that there is some worth
to this pain.

Night Owls

When a thought gets stuck in a loop,
it just goes on and on and on.
I try and distract myself,
but distractions only last for so long.

I try and escape it,
but I tend to believe my own lies.
I try and shut it down,
but I already know I'm not sleeping tonight.

Wonders to Worries

The questions you are most afraid to ask hold the
answers that are capable of altering your reality.
Just ask the questions already so as to close the period
of wondering.
Our minds have this way of over-analyzing wonders
and turning them into worries.

Never let wonders become worries because worries
can destroy you.

Innocence

Every morning
for just a while
I forget what's going on.

Hurts to say
I've been living this way
already for so long.

Cleanse

Sometimes, the tears come
because there have just been
too many moments,
tiny, painful moments
that have built up endlessly
and your mind is tired
of having to carry them all.

Saying Goodbye to My Grandmother

It has been written time and time again
that things will get better in the morning,
that the light will wash away
the clouded darkness in my mind…

Then death came and showed me
what it looked like,
and I took back all my colorful words of light
because death did not get better in the morning.

I had to learn and realize
that death is not the end,
nor is it the beginning.
It is one with life.

At the end of the day, life and death walk hand in hand
passing through every crevice of existence,
and the sooner we realize that we have no choice
but to face them both, the sooner we allow the light to
come through.

Before the Cliff

Do you ever get the feeling
that you're on the brink?

On the brink of madness,
on the brink of tears,
on the brink of inexplicable joy,
on the brink of rage –

It's coming, you know it's coming,
you can feel it coming, but it
never quite gets there.

Your eyes are widening,
your tears are welling up,
a smile is creeping in,
your cheeks are starting to burn –

then it floats away.
Gone.

Idle Bones

Oh I've been warned about
jealousy and greed,
pride and anger,
bitterness and holding grudges,
but my goodness

no one ever told me anything
about the sly and silent
eye of idleness
that seeps into your bones
halting your very urge
to go out and live.

Mediocrity

Living in the pursuit
of running away from who you are
is not living at all.

I lost myself and everything
slowly started to get very dull.

The wind only slightly caressed my arm,
the water barely ever quenched my thirst.
My bed faintly called me to sleep.
The food filled my mouth with hardly any taste.
Conversations very rarely moved me.

And that was not who I am,
but because I lost myself,
I lost my passion,
and when I lost my passion,
I settled for mediocre days.

That is what plummeted me to darkness.

Prison of Doubt

I'm going through the motions,
afraid to make the next move.
I'm paralyzed with the fear
of getting it all wrong.

But it doesn't stop,
not even for one bit.
Life keeps going anyway,
yet I'm stuck here like this.

It's hard to even think about it,
but I'll say it anyway –
I can hardly ever admit
that I'm terribly afraid.

Afraid of being trapped
somewhere I don't belong,
but by avoiding it more and more
I don't realize I've been trapping myself all along.

Agitation

Again, it's circling your mind,
your stubborn, stubborn mind.

>   You hate it,
>   but it's there,

and it stays for just awhile.

You can't explain it,
oh how badly you want it gone.
You wait and pray it's over,
and, as always, distractions get you through.

It goes away eventually.
It always goes away,
or at least that's what you tell yourself.
You can't bear for it to stay.

What We Hide

In reality,
you get eaten up
by the things
you try so hard
to hide.

Coming Undone

Sometimes it takes awhile
for me to become unhinged,
but other times it happens
so quickly, so suddenly,
so alarmingly out of the blue

that I wonder
if I've just become
so good at hiding the mess,
even from myself.

The Detriment of Memory

The tears come quick
and the darkness creeps in.
The memory lives on
because the pain was unspeakable.

One thought
and you are brought back
to the night
your life changed forever.

It only takes a second
of thinking about what once was,
and the flood of ache
returns rushing over you.

The Ego

You know this feeling is universal.
You know that others have felt this way
time and time again,
but when it is happening to you –
when this feeling overcomes your entire being –
it feels as though
you are the only one in the world
who is punished and made to feel it.

Thoughts of "Society"

More often than not,
the person you are
running away from
is yourself.

More often than not,
the person you try
so hard not to disappoint
is yourself.

More often than not,
the person you seek
constant approval from
is yourself.

It is just easier
to disguise this reality
by laying the blame on
your father, your friends,
even the infamous
figment of your imagination
that you call "Society".

Crawling Into Your Head

You are disconnected
from your roots
when you find yourself worried
about what goes on circling
in the minds of others.

Other People

When you make decisions
based on what you think
other people are thinking,
you will drain
your entire being
of the energy it needs
to live a meaningful life.

The Life of Tears

You worry and worry
when you can't say what needs to be said.

You have practiced over and over,
yet nothing comes out,
not when you need it to, not when it counts.

Sometimes, when you're unlucky,
it comes out in tears,
but tears don't always show what you feel.
You know it's a defense mechanism (but they don't).

You're scared, angry, and frustrated
but you're not sad.
No, you're not sad.

The tears betray you,
your lack of words betrays you
because you're not sad.
No, you're not sad,
but in the end, people remember what they see.

The Other Paths

I am being pushed
over the edge
by my own thoughts.

Scenarios are whirling,
gathering, building, revealing
to me all I've lost.

The world of possibilities
always tails me and taunts me,
willing my eyes shut.

Questioning my capabilities,
my mind flashes left and right
seeing glimpses of who I could've become.

Night Terrors

When my thoughts are loud enough
to wake me up in the middle of the night,
I try to tell myself that
they are just exaggerations of reality
and I must go back to sleep.

I try and tell myself that
they are just fleeting,
passing, impermanent,
and I must go back to sleep.

But these thoughts always tend to win
in the absence of the light,
and I can never seem to convince myself
that it will be better by morning.

When morning comes
it gets better, it always does,
but it's during the few hours of the night
that I can't find a way out
of my very own head.

Puppeteer

It's almost as though
all the strings
I had just recently
gotten the hang of holding
simultaneously slipped
from my fingers,
and I have no strength
to put them all back together.

Take a Break and Breathe

There's a dark cloud hovering over me,
and I don't quite know how to get rid of it

This has happened before,
and I know it will pass,
but it's difficult
when you can't yet see the light
at the end of the tunnel,
or the silver lining,
or a glimpse of that promised rainbow.

But deep down I know
the light is there,
it just needs a little break.

What You Must Face

When I can't bear the thought
of sitting alone at home
for an entire day,
I know I must.

I must sit and face
what I am running from,
or it will continue
to dictate my life.

Anxiety

The panic comes when I am thinking
of tomorrow, next week, next year,
ten years from now, or even later tonight.

The panic comes when I am thinking
about what he said, what she said,
or even what I may have said.

The panic comes when I am thinking
of what I should've done, what I could've done,
or what I would've done.

The panic comes when my mind
is anywhere other than
right here and right now.

Attachment

We hold on to circumstances like we own them,
we attach ourselves to people as if they were ours.

There must be a way to let go
without destroying a part of you...
I have to find that way.

I hold on.
I attach.
I crave control.

Take Back the Power

Look at whatever is bothering you straight in the eye, and I mean face it right down to its core. More often than not, you will see right through it and realize that only by avoiding it do you feed its strength.

A Speck of What Matters

I always wish to remain
in touch with what moves me –
there are so many distractions
to what truly matters,
and they disguise themselves to seem
much more important
than they really are.

I know, I understand
that it's so easy to be fooled
by these diversions,
but you must at least try
and see if there is even
a speck of what matters to you
in that cloud of distractions.

If there is a speck,
then focus on what matters.
It will help you get past
that which can be so difficult.
If there isn't, then try
and drop that burden completely.

Storms

A certain calm fills the Earth
when the clouds decide that the rain
is simply too heavy to bear.
These clouds, they let it all go.

Look at that,
look at what letting go can get you –
a release so great and freeing
that you are once again as light as air.

The Dressmaker

For quite some time,
she had been an unraveling seam,
and she learned the hard way
that seams don't unravel endlessly.

Finally, the seam fell apart,
and though she was broken,
there was nowhere to go other than
to stitch the cloth back together.

Then it dawned on her
that unraveling slowly
was a bigger burden
than just finally coming undone.

Away From Apathy

When everything slips away
and all you have left
is yourself,
you must feel.
Feel your way back home.

Feel the anger,
feel the pain,
feel the sadness,
then feel the light slowly start
to emerge from all the debris.

Forget everything else,
but you must always feel.

Seek Stillness

On the surface once again
and I can feel the waves
of frustration, madness,
failure, disappointment.

I know all I need to do
to see these things,
but not be swayed by them
is to dive in deep.

Down to the center
where there is stillness and silence
where not even a ripple
can move me from where I choose to float.

A Chance to Rise

You feel yourself slipping.
Slipping away from everything
you have ever known.

You are terrified
and opposed to change,
and this resistance is
what is making the journey
so much more difficult
than it has to be.

Do not resist the fall,
it may be the only way
to ever give yourself a chance
to finally rise once again.

Feel and Let Go

You must sit on the pain.
Give it the attention
it needs to be heard,
so that it can walk away
knowing that you have already learned.

Pain comes and startles you.
It wakes you up
from the monotonous
beat of existence.
It tells you that you are alive.

Return

Dive in
when the world is cold
and the night gets old,
dive in.

Dive in
when the memories rise,
and you can't sleep tonight,
dive in.

Dive in
when you feel alone
and you're losing it all,
dive in.

Dive in
to the stillness, the silence,
the deep well of who you are,
dive in

The Mantra

You are you are you are you.

When you are feeling helpless
and disconnected from the truth,
repeat this thought over and over
until you remember
that this is your life,
and only you really know
how to live it.

Hush

Hush, my child.
I know right now it's difficult
and it's not going exactly
the way you think it should.

Hush, my child.
I know you feel as though
there is so much to carry
and you are on your own.

Hush, my child.
Tonight is a night of rest
and when you let go for a while
you will realize

that the world will continue
to move and to spin
while you are taking the time
to finally take a deep breath.

In every inhale, breathe in clarity
and in every exhale, release doubt.
Hush, my child,
and let me guide your breath.

Still Waters

It all comes in waves. One moment you are drowning in all that is expected of you - the deadlines, the meetings, the errands - and you continue taking little sips of air, tired of having to move against the gushing water.

Then comes the stillness, it always follows. After all you have had to do, right now you can finally breathe because the waves have ceased. It's been a long time since you have relished in the calmness that comes with still waters, and finally, it is once again a joy to swim.

Plead to the Heavens

Let go of thoughts
you cannot control,
let them sort themselves out.

I had lost my way
countless times,
but I just walked on.

In times I could not
carry the weight,
I held my head up

and pleaded to the heavens,
to God, to the Universe -
help, I need your help.

Then, and only then,
when I acknowledged the burden
did it lift, along with all my worries.

Journey

M.B.Victoria

Do not strive for perfection,
that path will destroy you.
Instead, strive for truth.

Dawn

There is a stillness
in the morning
when the rain has slowed
to a drizzle.

The turmoil
of a difficult night
has settled, has rested,
has welcomed a fresh start.

Little by Little

Remember
that not everything
has to happen all at once.

Today is a piece of the puzzle.

The Pulse

Everything I have ever experienced
runs through me
like a pulse,
steady beats
that urge me to keep going.

These beats remind me
that there is a process,
that there are steps that must be taken
one by one
to get to where I want to be.

Nature Speaks

Whenever you feel lost and so utterly afraid,
just stop and take a quick break from life.
Watch a tree and see how its leaves
move so effortlessly and in perfect harmony.

The wind is what pushes these leaves,
and the leaves never put up a fight.
They move with the wind and not against it,
and the flow is mesmerizing.

Open yourself up to the forces
that govern this entire universe.
Accept and move along with all
that enchant this world.

M.B.Victoria

Life After Trauma

When you're tired of hearing
that *it's a pity you went through it,*
no one should go through that,
and *it's no wonder you're all bottled up,*

I am here to remind you
that while this is all true,
you hold the strength of a thousand warriors,
the heart of all the saints,
and the will to survive of a bird
about to take flight from its nest.

I am here to apologize
for the world that can be so cruel,
for some people who are made of wickedness,
and all the terrors you have felt.

I am here to tell you
that this earth does hold beauty,
that there are kind and gentle people,
and that you must allow yourself
to seek hope and freedom
because I promise you, it exists.

Finally, I am here to thank you
for being alive
because you are proof that out of extreme darkness
can emerge such a bright light.

Nostalgia

I am convinced all the more that we do remember it all.
The memories are stored in tiny boxes at the back of
our minds, but they are there. They will always be
there.

All it takes is for you to see someone that once played a
role in your life and the memories will fly out to the
forefront of your thoughts. Seeing that person again is
both beautiful and sad, I know.

The waves of nostalgia then run through your veins and
slowly they bring you back to where you are, but only
after reminding you what it took to get here.

Mother

After a night
of worrying, wanting,
and waiting,
the sunlight becomes
a savior, a mother,
and an awakening.

Soothe Your Soul

Find a rhythm
and settle yourself there
even for just awhile.

Let it soothe you,
calm your thoughts,
and bring you back to life.

Winding Road

The right path beckons me to follow it
because it knows that
I can only ever be truly alive
when I walk the road
that solely I am to pave.

Meditation

Everyone will be telling you
who you should and shouldn't be,
where you should and shouldn't go,
what you should and shouldn't do.

But you owe it to yourself
to listen to the still
and steady voice
inside your own being.

Without it, you will
forever be searching
for something
you might never find.

Action

It is easy to lose sight
of what you truly want
if your mind
is clouded with doubt.

You must seek clarity
and constantly
praise the path
that you are on

because it is this path
that will eventually
lead you to where
you want to be.

Welcome fear, but only
to the extent that it
will show you what is
important enough to pursue.

Immerse Yourself

It is overwhelming
to look at the big picture.
It isn't fair to stamp on
the pressure of the end goal
without completely immersing yourself
in every stage and each step
it will take for you
to finally get there.

Take Time to Marvel

It's a race, they say
and it does always feel like one
because you hear
and you hear and you hear,
but you do not listen.

You do not listen
to the whispers of your center
reminding you to walk –
to walk and to watch and to see.

It is not a race.
It is a walk where you can marvel at
all that is around you,
all that has gone by you,
and all that is coming your way.

Your Truth

The deeper I go into
all these distractions,
the farther away I am
from my own truth.

Walk On

It could be the steady beat
of you moving forward –

no matter how slowly,
how carefully, or how softly,
just continuous motion
despite all the opposition –

that will get you where
you truly want to be.

The Applause

I sit and wonder
if *this* is all going
to amount to something
in the very end.

Then it hits me
that life isn't about
a single grand finale.
The moments are what matter most
and *this* is all that really counts.

Ordinary People

Reality fascinates me –
the way people live
day in and day out
with all the quirks and worries,
laughter and struggles,
and yet we continue to go on
because that's life, isn't it?

The act of keeping on
keeping on.

Action Over Thoughts

The future houses infinite
potentials, but it is our
actions of today, not thoughts
of tomorrow that unlock
the realm of possibilities.

Stories of the Mind

The mind is as cunning
as it is kind,
but what emerges
depends on what
we surround it with.

Wisely choose
what you allow your mind
to be exposed to
because it is powerful enough
to change your life.

Hell and Heaven

My mind can take me
to hell and back
in a matter of seconds.

The same way that it can
show me heaven
in just a blink of an eye.

Fallen Leaves

People ask me
if it's ever possible
to give yourself
a second chance.

I ask them back
if they have ever
seen the fallen
leaves dance.

Invisible Guides

When you're on the brink of giving up,
circumstances will align in such a way
that you are exposed to someone or something
that reminds you why you started this,
and why you must continue
in the pursuit of that which can sometimes
seem so difficult.

The Limits You Create

The only limits that have
the power to stop you
are the limits
you set yourself.

You are the biggest hurdle
to your own potential,
and unless you realize that,
you will forever fear freedom.

The Only Way to Find It

As it has been said over and over –
you never find what you are looking for
simply because you
do not realize to turn inward.
To move the search from mountains and seas
to your very center and being.

What you seek lies hidden beneath
all the distractions, and all the motion.
It lies comfortably with
the silence you so foolishly fear.

Shift the Search Within

She searched for what she lacked everywhere she went.
Little did she know she could only find it within her,
and nowhere else.

Let Them Serve Their Purpose

Use the tears,
use the sadness,
use the anger
and point them all
towards the sky.

Wait for creativity
to come pouring down
and take it all.

You might as well
benefit from the pain
this experience is handing you.

Live A Little

All inspiration asks
is that you live a little,
so it can bring out
all that you have felt

and orchestrate it
into a tangible
piece of art.

The Myth of Perfect Timing

You go on waiting
and waiting
for circumstances to align
not knowing that
all you are really doing
is waiting for yourself.

How else do you think
opportunities arise?

You go and make
things happen.
You go and plant the seeds
needed for the
alignment of circumstance
and opportunities.

You are waiting for yourself
and no one else.

Reflections

All that you can see
are mirrors.
Everything (and everyone)
has the ability
to reveal to you
who you really are.

Look Up

There can never be silence because each chance she gets, the world whispers to us things we are usually not able to hear – rainfall on a quiet night, wind on a Sunday afternoon, and waves on a stormy day. We long for the idea of silence only because our souls crave for the presence of the universe. In the age we live in, to find peace becomes a challenge when it has been and will always be our instinct.

It Matters

You are nervous because it matters.
Do not resist the butterflies in your stomach,
your sweaty palms,
your jittery manner,
or your shifting eyes.

You are nervous because you know that
the event that is unfolding
will change your life in one way or another.

You are on edge, I know.
Accept it with open arms,
welcome the thoughts of what could be,
but do not let these thoughts rule you.
Welcome them, but also let them go.

You are nervous because it matters,
remember that.

Adventure

It is always easier
not to try new things,
but my god
that is the beginning
of the death of your soul.

To Understand

Sometimes words do not suffice when I am trying
to explain what's going on deep, deep down inside,
but that's fine... all that matters is that I feel it
and that I know that it is real, and it exists.

Sometimes even when words do suffice, people choose
not to try and understand what you're trying to say.
It's more convenient for them to stick to their beliefs,
and I am slowly learning to just let them be.

Sometimes people understand exactly what you're
saying, but they contradict your thoughts because
those thoughts threaten their very core and being,
and I have really been trying to accept this.

Sometimes there are those who understand you,
and are willing to listen to what you're saying.
Be grateful, do not take advantage of their gift.
They are the ones worth sharing your thoughts to.

Align

Sometimes it all works out perfectly well, and I can't
help but smile at the synchronicity of
my feelings, my thoughts, my words, and the
conversation.
It is rare, but at least I know it exists.

Choose Happiness

Happily, I have wandered.
Happily, I have stumbled,
Happily, I have risen.
Happily, I continue to live.

Open Palm

Do not strive to keep happiness
because you are broken when it is lost.

Let it flow freely through your veins,
let it come and let it leave.

When it is there just feel it,
feel it without the interference of thoughts.

Photographs of Life

Blink. The bell rings, class is over.
Blink. You receive your diploma.
Blink. It's a hard day, you want so badly to rest.
Blink. You got it, you got the job!
Blink. "You may kiss the bride."
Blink. The baby is crying again.
Blink. You're on the road, windows down, smiles all around.
Blink. They're all over for Sunday lunch.
Blink. Silence.
Blink. Blink. Blink.

Beautiful Exhaustion

Your body will always reach
a point of exhaustion,
but if you enjoy what you are doing
then in that tiredness, you will breathe
a sigh of relief, not regret.

Here is to hoping that we live a life
with more sighs of relief.

Close Your Eyes To See

Close your eyes for just a while.
Do you feel it?
Not yet, I suppose, but if you just
remember to close your eyes for just awhile,
soon you will feel it loud and clear.

You will feel the slight touch
of the wind across your cheek.
You will suddenly realize that
there are birds chirping nearby.
You will notice an emptiness in your mind
that will, at first, scare you,
but slowly you will come to realize
how pleasant it is to be free of thoughts.
You will accept the silence
that is falling on you,
and you will then see that closing your eyes
only lets you see so much clearer.

To Grow

In the space between
what you are comfortable with
and what you are afraid to try
lies the beauty
that comes with growth.

The Energy

I feel it,
I feel it once again
at the very tips of my fingers.
I feel the energy of potential
running through my veins.

I am here, I am whole,
I am who I am,
and after a long while,
I am once again thrilled
at the thought of what lies ahead.

The Falls in April

The hardest part
of every jump
is the moment right before
you finally take the plunge.

Becoming

I am learning
      to sit quietly
      and absorb.
I am learning
      to be patient
      and let it all in.
I am learning
      to make mistakes
      and then move on.
I am learning
      to listen to the soul
      and to put everything else aside.
I am learning
      to give love,
      and to take it.
I am leaning
      to pay attention to who I am
      and who I am becoming.
I am learning
      to live with my passion
      as the forefront of everything that I do.

Passion

Passion can propel you to places.
All it asks of you is that you let it.

Realms

We have to start
thinking of our lives
as realms of infinite possibilities.

Life is where our
decisions of today
shape our tomorrows.

That may seem daunting at first,
but when we realize the control we have
over our tomorrows,
we can start moving in a way that takes us
to brighter days.

Disney Fireworks

I call on
the child I once was,
I tell her to come over.
Come here quickly.

Bring your dreams,
your laughter,
your heart.
Bring them to me.
I will wrap them in my arms,

and I promise you
I will try
with all I have
to bring them to life.

The Law

We dream the dreams
That turn into something real.
What we think, we become;
We are what we feel.

The Fire

You're worried because of how much you want it,
but this time don't let your mind get in the way.
Just do it.
Do what you love to do,
and do it the way only you know how.

This isn't for anything else besides
that fire that burns within you.
That fire that never stops illuminating
all that you are made of.

There.

Do it for that fire
because it is the only thing that
drives you past the limits
of your own imagination.

It is a Part of You

It's so easy to drop in the back burner something that is difficult to pursue. It's so easy to make yourself forget about the wonders it can bring you. But the second you dip your foot in it once again, it becomes frighteningly impossible to keep lying to yourself because you are so intertwined with it, and as much as you hate to admit it, you know that you are rooted in it.

Light

First, you must believe in yourself.
Find that Light within you,
that Light which never goes out.

No matter what challenges or struggles arrive,
that Light will go on burning.
No matter how hard you try to ignore it,
it will have no end
because it has been in you since the beginning.

That Light has existed before this life,
and it will go on burning beyond it.
Trust it with all that you are.

Your Life Source

Find your escape.
Find that vein that
is able to connect you
to the universal voice.

Listen to it,
and keep it alive.

Her Secrets

The word is full of secrets
that she is willing to share
with those who choose to listen.

The greats of the past
sought for the truth
beyond what they thought they knew.

Be open to what comes your way.
As they say, empty your cup
to make room for truth.

Live While You Are Alive

It is unbelievably easy to coast by,
but that would be a complete disservice
to the surge of potential that courses through you.

This energy from existence seeks to create,
to excel, to become all that it can possibly be,
but this can only be done if you choose
to take this potential and challenge it to expand.

It is easy to choose mediocrity,
but it is also so difficult
to die with the potential still urging
and roaring and begging you to stay alive.

Give Yourself Completely

Whatever it is you are doing,
give yourself completely.
Be so immersed in it
that when you are done,
you are done.

It is only when we do things
mindlessly that we end up
looking back and wondering
where we would be
if we had given it our all.

The Fear of Failure

There is no greater hindrance to living a fulfilling life than the fear of failure.

A Medium

There are times,
for no apparent reason,
my mind and body align
with a longing to create.

I become but a vessel
that allows the pulse
of the universe
to beat through me.

Why You Do What You Do

You create
in order to
extend the life
of a thought
that would have so quickly
fluttered away.

Pay Attention

Your creativity is like a muscle
that you must attend to.
Some days it will be difficult,
almost as though you have forgotten
how to move with it.

Other days it will be effortless.
Almost as though inspiration
itself has taken you by the hand
and led you to the
very essence of existence.

Soul River

In all that you do,
let your soul flow through you.

The Creator

You are a creator,
your heart beats for stories.

You are a creator,
you live and die a thousand times.

You are a creator,
a teardrop holds the entire world.

You are a creator,
you bleed paint, or words, or notes.

You are a creator,
and it is both a burden and a blessing
that you are so connected to this life

because your creations can so quickly move you
from inspiration to despair,
and rarely is there anything in between.

The Universe in Me

Something moves within me,
it never stops and it never sleeps.

I have learned to welcome it
because it will stay anyway.

I have grown to move with it,
and to listen when it calls me.

Some say it is my soul, energy, my being,
I think it is all three and more.

It may be the universe, the entire universe;
there must be pieces of the universe within me.

Slowly I am learning that sometimes
the universe craves to express.

Slowly I am understanding
that my body is merely a medium,

a medium that must listen
in order to create.

Ablaze

Maybe it was at that exact moment
that it dawned on me that I am no longer
afraid to live my life the way I want to.
I am no longer afraid to sit and marvel
at my very own thoughts.

There is only my path to follow,
and I would rather burn than crawl
on someone else's footsteps.

Daughters

We are fighting because
we have been so carelessly placed
inside labeled boxes taped shut.

We are fighting because
we have been living in bodies
and judged accordingly.

We are fighting because
we have been told to stay home,
or that staying home means we are worthless.

We are fighting because
we have been stripped off of
the power to live the way we want to.

Finally, we are fighting because
though there are massive cracks in the glass ceiling,
it hasn't been completely shattered yet.

Magic

Watching her work
was like watching someone
conduct an entire orchestra
without even lifting a finger.

It was magic, really.

Transform

The present is laced with promise
and it is up to us
to take it, to hone it, to transform it
into something that can eventually
give us the power
to not only make choices,
but also to stand by them
without the fear of losing our freedom.

Get Up and Go

A day is a day,
darling,
until you choose
to make something of it.

Even Just a Little

You give bits of your energy
to people, hoping
they will take it
and run with it
to make the world

just a little brighter,
just a little safer,
just a little kinder.

Pursuing Your Passion

Even though you are tired,
broken,
and half asleep,
it isn't work for you –
it's what you live for.

Wonderstruck

Sometimes you feel something
so powerful that you desperately
seek out the words
that will enable you to
immortalize the moment,
but such grand moments
choose to leave you
with nothing but
waves of awe.

Sometimes, and I mean
really just a few times,
even words are not worthy
to grasp what has just
rushed through you.

The Shifts

One minute you feel
tiny and inconsequential –
not even a player in the game,

and the next you feel
that every inch of your being
is brimming with purpose.

Oh how quickly the mind
can take over the narrative
of any story.

Whole

Feed your inspiration,
your creativity,
your wonder.

Feed your enthusiasm,
your passion,
your awe.

Feed all that can
make you feel
like you are living.

This will silence the thoughts,
and remind you
that you are always enough.

Grace

To live a life
of healing and grace,
we must walk lightly.

We must leave behind
what can weigh us down
and continue to move forward.

Beauty in the Mundane

There is magic in the ordinary,
there is beauty in the plain.
Just look, and soon you will see
nothing is ever the same.

All

It's just one moment. Just give yourself, every fiber of your being to that one moment. It exists only through you, so you must live entirely in it. If you live in it, then that moment's existence will matter.

Our Skin

How thrilling would it be
to be so comfortable in your own skin
that every movement is effortless
and free of any calculation?

A Day Fully Lived

I am tired.
No, it's not the tired
that's defeated and disappointed.

It's the tired that
runs through my veins as I
appreciate a cozy bed.

It's the tired
that tells me I have
done all I could.

It's the tired
that puts me straight to sleep
without thoughts whirling about.

It's the tired
that finally means a day
well and fully lived.

Human Soul

Watching people do
what they love to do
never fails to leave me in awe
of the glorious capacity of the human soul
to accomplish things so wonderfully.

Those people who live their lives
in the pursuit of their passions
are the majesties of this Earth,
and they house the spirits
that contribute to the life of the Universe.

This

Remember this feeling, the feeling that completely takes over you. No matter how difficult it gets, or no matter how stagnant it can become, keep pushing because this feeling of pure delight and love for what you do does surface. It is worth every doubt and every manifestation of fear because this passion exists.

Sunday Afternoons

Have you ever found yourself
lying in bed on a Sunday afternoon
exactly when the sun
slowly starts to descend
warning you that it won't
be seeing you until tomorrow?

And although you're usually
miserable when this is happening,
this time an overwhelming
sense of possibility washes over you –

The realization that there are
infinite versions of reality
that can transpire,
and you are capable of making decisions
that will result in the birth
of the reality that is today,

the reality that matters most,
the reality that is now.

Gold

Take your energy and your being
wherever you go.
You'll paint the world
with bursts of your very own gold.

A Speck

No, it's not about surviving
until each milestone.
It's about living
so completely
that a milestone becomes
just a speck
in your vibrant existence.

Overflow

Today, I will give.
I will give to those who need
and I will give to those who
do not yet know that they need.

I will give and give
until exhaustion
courses through my veins
and tells me I have done my part,

that I have given enough
to show the world that I am here
and that it can trust
that I am willing to truly live.

To Begin Your Rest

Sometimes it worries me
that I will no longer
have anything left to say,
but then I am slowly realizing
that if I ever get to that point,
It may turn out to be
a giant sigh of relief.

A relief in that I have finished –
I have said all that needed to be said,
and at that moment,
I will have begun my rest.

Returning

When you are close
to getting what you want,
fear will try and distract you.

When this happens,
you must hold your fear,
and gently remind it

that you are simply
on your way home -
somewhere you have always known.

Home

*In moments of
absolute mess and turmoil,
I must turn inward
and know that I am home.
I am always home.*

Unearth the Softness

Maybe you buried the softness
for fear of being caught off-guard.
The softness now lies underneath
the walls and steel barriers
that are meant to protect you
from vulnerability, from being seen.

But, my darling, you forget
that in softness is grace,
light, spirit, comfort, and love.
Now, hiding the softness
does keep it from the world,
but it also keeps it from you.

Unveiling You

The balance has been restored
and I feel as though
the pieces of myself that have
long stayed in hiding
are slowly revealing
themselves to me.

I am thankful
that they see the comfort
I have now allowed myself
to finally feel.

In You is What You See

If there is kindness
in your eyes,
you will see kindness
in others.

Do what you must
to cultivate that kindness.

It might mean having to
forgive yourself for the
mistakes you might have made.

It might mean letting go
of the ideas
you think define you.

It might mean finding the strength
to shed from the protection
of who you thought you were.

As Your Eyes Open

When the day
hasn't yet begun
and no one is awake,
not even the sun,
take it upon yourself
to breathe deeply
and give thanks
for all that is to come.

It Is You

In the stillness
I heard a voice
that told me everything
was the way it was supposed to be.

In the stillness
I heard a voice
that reminded me I was whole.

In the stillness
I heard that same voice
that I recognized
was my very own.

Excitement

These emotions are overwhelming.
Sometimes they come and I can't control them –
my heart beats too quickly,
and I can't explain why.

It's not an unpleasant feeling,
the excitement that pulses through my veins.
This may be some sort of premonition
of the coming of better days.

I close my eyes and waves
of happiness move through me.

I don't know what it is,
I don't know why it's here,
but I welcome it anyway.

This might be what it means
to live without thinking, without expectations,
and just going through each day
with unending thanks.

With the Current

Have you ever tried
swimming against the current?
It is exhausting.

How did you feel
when you finally let go?
It is freeing.

I have been
resisting life
for far too long.

I now choose
to be present
and just listen.

Centered

A wave of calm
washes over me
when I settle myself
in the arms of the present.

Passenger Seat

I found myself
watching the world go by,
and despite all the noise,
movement,
and chaos,

I felt the stillness
and the silence
underneath it all.

Receive

It is only when you are
where you are
at the moment you are there
that you are able to take
what life has been
trying so hard to hand you.

Deep Well Within

In my case,
inspiration doesn't come
from anywhere else,
other than deep within me.

Something may happen
that will cause the inspiration
to bubble up and come alive,
but it is already there –
it has always been there.

Nothing external can affect you
if a part of it doesn't already exist in you.

Exquisiteness

The thing is that
I have grown accustomed
to this or that, black or white,
yes or no, win or lose.

It is only once in awhile
that it dawns on me
that life does not have to
consist of polar opposites.

The exquisiteness of life
lies in the possibilities
that are unveiled to me
little by little.

It is not this or that, but all.
It is not black or white, but a spectrum.
It is not yes or no, but "I will try."
It is not win or lose, but I have learned.

As long as I am accepting,
the opportunities will come,
and when they come,
I know it is all working out.

Peel the Layers

It is only when I know
that eyes aren't watching,
ears aren't listening,
and minds aren't judging
that I can peel off every layer
I have so carefully wrapped
around who I really am.

Temples of Cambodia

Words do not suffice, words never suffice the need
to capture the awe I feel when in the presence of the
divine.
No, I don't mean gods and goddesses, well at least
I don't mean the gods and goddesses that you talk
about.

I mean the divine that is stillness and movement;
the divine that is within and around you;
the divine that governs both heaven and hell;
the divine that embraces and shuns you;
the divine that is both creation and destruction;
the divine that is inspiration and emptiness;
the divine that is infinite and non-existent;
the divine that is life and death.

It is only through awareness that
I am brought back to the center,
and it is only in the center that
I get a glimpse of the divine.

In the Flesh

I hope to one day realize
that I myself
am a manifestation
of the Universe in the flesh.

Droplets

Ultimately, at the very root of us all,
we will find out that each of us is a droplet from the
same source.
Not just humans, but every single thing that lives is a
droplet from the whole, a droplet from existence
herself.

Sacred Feminine

My body is the house
in which my children
will reside.

I must care for it
in such a way that it will hold them
and raise them properly, perfectly.

Worth of the Flow

There is a flow within and around us.
When we are in sync, life is easy and so beautiful,
but when we are out of sync
it almost feels as though we are constantly trekking
uphill –
going through the same motions,
just with so much resistance.

Find ways to get back in the flow.
It takes effort, but the flow is worth it all.

Give and Take

There are mornings
when something just clicks,
and the rhythm you thought
you had already lost
falls right back into place.

The little fragments
of who you have become
fuse back together
to make it so that
you are whole once again.

You still remember
all that you have lost,
but you also understand
that in losing, you have gained
all you have today.

Smile, My Love

Sitting by the edge of the bed,
staring at the clouds
thinking of all that's transpired,
of everything that's gone down.

Remembering what it took to get here,
feeling all I've felt.
Knowing this all led me
right back to myself.

Watching the rain finally patter,
hearing the clouds break free.
Wondering what else is meant to come
finding its way to me.

Smiling at the thought of life
working out just fine.
In awe of the revelation that
what I had once wanted is now mine.

Daydreams

Being there with everyone else,
I finally understood
what it was like to feel at home.

It is not a house,
or even other people...
It is to be so comfortable
and at peace with yourself
that nothing external
can affect you without your permission.

Back to the Center

For the first time in months,
I was able to sit still
on my own with no distractions.
My mind was not screaming
a thousand thoughts simultaneously.
My body was not racing
to be somewhere else –
anywhere else, just not alone.

I was back to my center,
I was back to my self.

Rest

There is a certain loveliness
to the slow, steady hum
that sometimes occurs
on a cold Saturday morning.

All that has passed
and all that is up ahead
seem to pause for a bit,
hanging on a balance.

Finally, there is time
to rest from all you have done
and smile about
everything that is yet to come.

Likeness

Whether your skin
is white enough,
dark enough,
or clear enough –

Whether your hair
is long enough,
short enough,
or straight enough –

Whether your eyes
are big enough,
green enough,
or brown enough –

Whether your smile
is wide enough,
fixed enough,
or charming enough –

None of these matter
if the light within you
is not bright enough,
not vibrant enough,
or not free enough.

Focus on that light
because if you give it
even half of the attention
that you give your outer self,

then I promise you
you will be enough,
you will be more than enough.
You have the ability to enchant the world.

Lessons From Your Mother

Child, the earth
is constantly calling for you
to listen to what is essential.

Dust yourself off of
the mindless chatter of others,
it can only weigh you down.

Remember the truth
whispered by your own mother –
you are love in the flesh.

Pieces of You

I am made up
of all the books I've read,
people I've spoken to,
stories I've heard,
and scenarios I've witnessed.

I am a compilation
of ideas, thoughts, and hopes.
I am built on history,
fashioned by the efforts
of my father,
and the strength
of my mother.

But in the center
there is a beat -
steady, steady, always the same -
that has been in me
and will remain with me
long after everything else
has slowly slipped away.

Permission

Allow yourself to breathe,
allow yourself not to think about
any form of direction your life must take.

Allow yourself to laugh,
allow yourself to forget about
everything that is currently at stake.

Allow yourself to wonder,
allow yourself to get lost in a story
that tells you "soon it will all make sense."

Allow yourself to smile,
allow yourself to realize how simple,
but monumental it is that you are here.

What You Thought You'd Forgotten

I can hear life once again –
the rustle of the leaves,
the breath of the dog,
the chirp of a cricket,
and the laughter of a child.

For a while I think
I closed myself off to life
because I was too busy
fighting with my thoughts.

Now I can hear it all.
Now I can breathe.
Now I know I am living.

Where You Are

A calm washed over me,
and right then and there I knew
that I was exactly where
I was supposed to be.

This thought consumed me
from inside out,
and I couldn't help but praise
everything that had
ever happened in my life
because how else
could everything about this day
have fallen right into place?

Enchantment

I'm a mess
I'm difficult
I'm all over the place
I'm indecisive
I'm self-destructive,

and yet

I am laughter
I am happiness
I am enchantment
I am wonder
I am whole.

The Silence

Remember that amidst all the noise,
there is an infinite silence at your very center.
A silence that no one, not even you, can infiltrate.

Participate, Live

Find the pleasure in
participating totally
in everyday life.

Find the magic in
the trivial actions
performed day in and day out.

Find the beauty in
the motion
of all fixed routines.

Be there – awake,
alive, aware in
each and every moment.

I am.

That is quite possibly
the most powerful sentence
you will ever utter.

With just those
two words,
you are centered.

Nothing precedes it,
nothing comes after –
you simply are.

Listen

Now tell me, have you
ever really listened?

The wind is trying to
remind you to breathe.
The deep breath of the belly,
not the shallow, nervous
breaths of the chest.

The birds are trying to
remind you to sing.
Songs from your very own center,
sing them loud and clear
without any fear.

The leaves are trying to
remind you to dance
the rhythm that longs to be
released, finally let them
free without any hesitation.

The clouds are trying to
remind you to move.
Move without resistance
towards the path you are
and have always been drawn to.

Now tell me, have you
ever really listened?

Little One

Little one,
if I were to tell you
of all that's to come,
you wouldn't believe it.
No, you wouldn't believe it.

Frankly, if I were to tell you
of all that's to come,
you would be in tears,
overwhelmed by the enormity
of all that is to transpire.

Your head would fill with rage
at the thought of how the universe
seems to always be out to get you.
How you never seem to be able
to just catch a tiny break.

But also your heart would fill with hope
at the thought of how the universe
seems to know when it's time
to pick you up gently,
and remind you that you are still well.

You might think as though
it would all be too much to handle,
and sometimes it is all too much,
but you make it through.
Sometimes with tears, other times with a smile.

I can happily tell you
that where you are today
is so beautiful.
You are making it,
and you are well.

There are bound to be difficult moments up ahead,
but you will make it.
You've always made it.
These moments, you will eventually learn,
make you exactly who you are.

I wish I could hold your hand
and let you know it will turn out well
even when everything seems to be falling apart.
Little one, I wish I could go back
and carry your entire world.

But I can't
because I am you, and if I were to go back,
I would be just as small and just as lost,
so all I can do, little one, is just promise you
that all will be well one day. All will be well.

Acknowledgments

I would like to thank...

My mom and dad, for handing me the journal when I was 7 years old that sparked my passion for words, and for being there for me every step of the way since.

My brother, for constantly provoking in me equal parts laughter and business ideas.

My sister, for showing me the true essence of patience, gratitude, and love.

My dearest friends, for the feedback and encouragement.

Most of all, my readers turned friends, for supporting me from the very beginning.

About the Author

M.B.Victoria is a writer and history teacher. You can keep in touch with her through her Instagram: @m.b.victoria.

.

Made in the USA
Las Vegas, NV
03 September 2021

29545946R00105